Follow Your Dreams

You Can If You Think You Can

▧ HAZELDEN®
Keep Coming Back™

Created by Meiji Stewart

Illustrated by David Blaisdell

Follow Your Dreams
© 2000 by Meiji Stewart

ISBN# 1-56838-514-5

Hazelden
P.O. Box 176
15251 Pleasant Valley Road
Center City, MN 55012-0176
1-800-328-9000
www.hazelden.org

Illustration: David Blaisdell, Tucson, Arizona
Cover design: Kahn Design, Encinitas, California

Dedicated to:
Marshall Rosenberg, the founder of the Center for Nonviolent
Communication (CNVC) and to all those who help share his message.
Marshall's language of compassion enriches my life daily and empowers
me to follow my dreams beyond anything I could have ever imagined.
Please visit www.cnvc.org for more information about his work.

Thanks to:
David for the wonderful illustrations. I was blessed to be able to work with
him. Thanks also to Roger and Darryl for putting it all together, almost
always under deadline (usually yesterday). Thanks to Jeff for the beautiful
book cover (front and back) and even more for his and Pete's friendship.
Thanks to Gay, Jane, Regina, Zane, and especially Neill for making it
possible to bring this book to life. Special thanks to my soul mate, Claudia,
my daughter, Malia, and stepson, Tommy, for teaching me how to love and
laugh lots and not take life too seriously...as do Star, Oliver, and Jewel.

I am where I am because I believe in all possibilities.

Whoopi Goldberg

Far away there in the sunshine are my highest
aspirations. I may not reach them, but I can look up
and see their beauty, believe in them and try to
follow where they may lead.

Louisa May Alcott

It's time to start living the life we've imagined.
Henry James

Cherish your visions, your ideals, the music that stirs in your heart. If you remain true to them, your world will at last be built.

James Allen

Great works are performed, not by strength but by perseverance.

Johann Wolfgang von Goethe

Destiny is not a matter of chance, it is a matter of choice. It is
not a thing to be waited for; it is a thing to be achieved.
William Jennings Bryan

That I am here is a wonderful mystery
to which I will respond with joy.

Every day is my best day; this is my life;
I'm not going to have this moment again.

Bernie Siegel

8

I never lose sight of the fact that just being is fun.
Katharine Hepburn

We all have possibilities we don't know about.
We can do things we don't even dream we can do.

Dale Carnegie

No pessimist ever discovered the secrets of the stars,
or sailed to an uncharted land, or opened a new
heaven to the human spirit.

Helen Keller

Ain't no chance if you don't take it. *Guy Clark*

I asked of life: What have you to offer me?
And the answer came: What have you to give?

I finally figured out the only reason to be alive
is to enjoy it.

Rita Mae Brown

Life truly is a boomerang. What you give, you get.
Dale Carnegie

Be brave enough to live creatively. The creative is the place where no one else has ever been. You have to leave the city of your comfort and go into the wilderness of your intuition. You can't get there by bus, only by hard work, risking, and by not quite knowing what you're doing. What you'll discover will be wonderful: yourself.

Alan Alda

The important thing is not to stop questioning. Curiosity has its own reason for existing....Never lose a holy curiosity.
Albert Einstein

Feel the fear and do it anyway.

Susan Jeffers

If you're alive, you've got to flap your arms and legs, you've got to jump around a lot, you've got to make a lot of noise, because life is the very opposition of death...if you're quiet, you're not living. You've got to be noisy, or at least your thoughts should be noisy and colorful and lively.

Mel Brooks

The purpose of life is to matter, to count,
to stand for something, to have it make some
difference that we have lived at all.

Leo Buscaglia

Life is what I make it,
always has been, always will be.

Grandma Moses

Dare to...

*A*sk for what you want.
*B*elieve in yourself.
*C*hange your mind.
*D*o what you love.
*E*njoy each and every day.
*F*ollow your heart's desire.
*G*ive more than you receive.
*H*ave a sense of humor.
*I*nsist on being yourself.
*J*oin in more.
*K*iss and make up.
*L*ove and be loved.
*M*ake new friends.

*N*urture your spirit.
*O*vercome adversity.
*P*lay more.
*Q*uestion conformity.
*R*each for the stars.
*S*peak your truth.
*T*ake personal responsibility.
*U*nderstand more, judge less.
*V*olunteer your time.
*W*alk through fear.
*X*perience the moment.
*Y*earn for grace.
be *Z*any.

© *Meiji Stewart*

Make voyages. Attempt them. There's nothing else.
Tennessee Williams

This life is a test. If it were a real life,
you would receive instructions on where to go
and what to do.

The rainbow is more beautiful than
the pot at the end of it.

Hugh Prather

Life is not a dress rehearsal—every day is opening night.
Peter Daniels

It is easy to sit up and take notice.
What is difficult is getting up
and taking action.

Al Batt

The real voyage of discovery consists not
in seeking new landscapes,
but in having new eyes.

Marcel Proust

You whose day it is, make it beautiful.
Get out your rainbow colors, so it will be beautiful.
Nootka Song to Bring Fair Weather

Realizing little dreams helps to have faith
in having big dreams.

Virginia Satir

We are such stuff as dreams are made of.

William Shakespeare

Life is not what you find, it's what you create.

You are today where your thoughts have brought you; you will be tomorrow where your thoughts take you.

James Allen

You have a unique message to deliver, a unique song to sing, a unique act of love to bestow. This message, this song, and this act of love have been entrusted exclusively to the one and only you.

John Powell

I change myself, I change the world. *Gloria Anzaldua*

If you are to be, you must begin by
assuming responsibility.

Richard Bach

You are the one person for whom you are entirely
responsible. Your world, your life can be better only
if you make it so. As you improve yourself, you
influence all others around you. Keep in mind that
you came into this life with a purpose to perform.

Harold Sherman

You can't hoot with the owls at night and fly with the eagles during the day.

Your life is like a book. The title page is your name; the preface, your introduction to the world. The pages are a daily record of your efforts, trials, pleasures, discouragements. Day by day your thoughts and acts are being inscribed in your book of life. Hour by hour, the record is being made that must stand for all time. One day the word "finis" must be written. Let it then be said of your book that it is a record of noble purpose, generous service and work well done.

Grenville Kleiser

Your world is as big as you make it.

Georgia Douglas Johnson

Do not compare yourself with others, for you are a
unique and wonderful creation. Make your own
beautiful footprints in the snow.

Barbara Kimball

Just when I found the meaning of life,
they changed it.

George Carlin

Take your mind out every now and then
and dance on it. It is getting all caked up.

Mark Twain

If you want to make an easy job seem mighty
hard, just keep putting it off.

Do what you love. Know your own bone.
Gnaw at it, bury it, unearth it, and gnaw it still.

Henry David Thoreau

People talk about finding their lives.
In reality, your life is not something you find—
it's something you create.

David Phillips

Be yourself. Who else is better qualified? *Frank J. Giblin II*

There are periods when to dare
is the highest wisdom.

William Ellery Channing

If you have a dream, give it a chance to happen.

Richard de Vos

Enthusiasm is nothing more or less than faith in action.
Henry Chester

Dreams don't work unless you do.

Peter Daniels

Any life is an unfinished story.

Ron Palmer

Imagination is the preview of life's coming attractions.
Larry Eisenberg

Enjoy yourself. It's later than you think.

Chinese Proverb

Just to be is a blessing. Just to live is holy.

Abraham Heschel

Normal day, let me be aware of the treasure you are.

Life is not short; life is eternal, so there is no question of any hurry. By hurrying you can only miss. In existence do you see any hurry? Seasons come in their time, flowers come in their time, trees are not running to grow fast because life is short. It seems as if the whole existence is aware of the eternity of life.

Osho

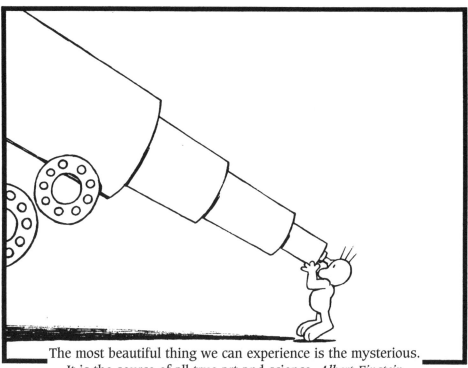

The most beautiful thing we can experience is the mysterious.
It is the source of all true art and science. *Albert Einstein*

If you don't like the scene you're in, if you are unhappy, if you're lonely, if you don't feel that things are happening, change your scene. Paint a new backdrop. Surround yourself with new actors. Write a new play—and if it's not a good play, get off the stage and write another one. There are millions of plays—as many as there are people.

Leo Buscaglia

Every man's work, whether it be literature,
or music, or pictures, or architecture, or anything
else, is always a portrait of himself.

Samuel Butler

I am only one, but still I am one. I cannot do
everything, but still I can do something.
And because I cannot do everything, I will not
refuse to do the something that I can do.

Helen Keller

45

Creativity Is...

Awakening your genius.
Being alive in the moment.
Cultivating change and curiosity.
Dreaming, dabbling, and daring.
Exploring infinite possibilities.
Fostering "trains of thought."
Going back to the drawing board.
Hard work and having fun too.
Indulging in your potential.
Joyful intensity and wild abandon.
Kindling your uniqueness.
Letting go of inhibitions.
Mindfulness and magic.

Never giving up on your dreams.
On- and off-the-wall thinking.
Playing, prospecting, and perusing.
Questioning and brainstorming.
Reading between the lines.
Soaring on your imagination.
Transcending the traditional.
Using all of your senses.
Visualizing the impossible.
Wallowing in wonder.
Xperiencing paradigm shifts.
Yearning for intuitive guidance.
Zestful zigzagging and zaniness.

© Meiji Stewart

There is no greater joy than of feeling oneself a creator. The triumph of life is expressed by creation. *Henri Bergson*

Wake up with a smile and go after life.
Live it, enjoy it, taste it, smell it, feel it.

Joe Knapp

Most people are as happy as they make up
their minds to be.

Abraham Lincoln

Do not be too timid and squeamish about your actions.
All life is an experiment. *Ralph Waldo Emerson*

Whatever you want to do, do it now.
There are only so many tomorrows.

Michael Landon

Each of us makes his own weather,
determines the color of the skies in the
emotional universe which he inhabits.

Fulton J. Sheen

50

If you're too busy to laugh, you're too busy, period.
Janet Meyer

Be not simply good; be good for something.

Henry David Thoreau

There are those of us who are always about to live.
We are waiting until things change, until there is
more time, until we are less tired, until we get a
promotion, until we settle down—until, until, until.
It always seems as if there is some major event that
must occur in our lives before we begin living.

George Sheehan

To find in ourselves what makes life worth living is risky business, for it means that once we know we must seek it. It also means that without it life will be valueless. *Marsha Sinetar*

To overcome difficulties is to experience
the full delight of existence.

Arthur Schopenhauer

There is nothing more beautiful than a rainbow, but
it takes both rain and sunshine to make a rainbow.
If life is to be rounded and many-colored like the
rainbow, both joy and sorrow must come to it.

You must know for which harbor you are headed if you are to catch the right wind to take you there. *Seneca*

Jump into the middle of things,
get your hands dirty,
fall flat on your face,
and then reach for the stars.

Joan L. Curcio

Think you can, think you can't;
either way you'll be right.

Henry Ford

It's not whether you get knocked down. It's whether you get up again. *Vince Lombardi*

Take a look at your natural river. What are you?
Stop playing games with yourself....
Where's your river going?
Are you riding with it?
Or are you rowing against it?...
Don't you see that there is no effort
if you're riding with your river?

Carl Frederick

Our main task is to give birth to ourselves.

Erich Fromm

You have enormous untapped power that you will probably never tap, because most people never run far enough on their first wind to ever find they have a second.

William James

When you do the best you can, you never know what miracle is wrought in your life, or in the life of another.

Helen Keller

There came a time when the risk to remain
tight in a bud was more painful than the risk
it took to blossom.

Anaïs Nin

Life's challenges are not supposed to paralyze you,
they're supposed to help you discover who you are.

Bernice Johnson Reagon

There comes a time when everyone has to lift
the horse's tail and face reality. *Oscar Wilde*

Listening to your heart is not simple.
Finding out who you are is not simple.
It takes a lot of hard work and courage to
get to know who you are and what you want.

Sue Bender

There's only one answer to the Mystery of Life.
You do as much of it as you can.

Spike Milligan

A man should hear a little music, read a little poetry, and see
a fine picture every day of his life, in order that worldly
cares may not obliterate the sense of the beautiful which God
has implanted in the human soul. *Johann Wolfgang von Goethe*

Life moves pretty fast; if you don't stop and
look around every once in a while,
you could miss it.

Ferris Bueller

It takes vision and courage to create—
it takes faith and courage to prove.

Owen D. Young

The willingness to do creates the ability to do.
Peter McWilliams

To raise new questions, new possibilities,
to regard old problems from a new angle,
requires creative imagination.

Albert Einstein

Let us go, now, and wake up our luck.

Cyprian Proverb

The atmosphere of expectancy is the breeding ground for miracles. *Rodney L. Parsley*

A person cannot travel within and
stand still without.

James Allen

The years in your life are less important than
the life in your years.

Ralph Waldo Emerson

One way to get the most out of life is to look upon it as an adventure. *William Feather*

It is said that sheep may get lost simply by nibbling away at the grass and never looking up. That can be true for any of us. We can focus so much on what is immediately before us that we fail to see life in larger perspective.

Donald Bitsberger

Dare to dream, dare to try, dare to fail—
dare to succeed.

G. Kinsley Wood

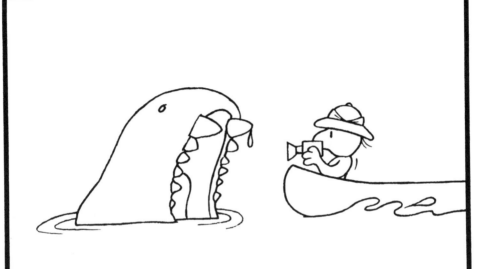

If we do not change our direction, we are likely to end up where we are headed. *Donald Bitsberger*

Life's a pretty precious and wonderful thing.
You can't sit down and let it lap around you...
you have to plunge into it; you have to dive
through it! And you can't save it, you can't store
it up; you can't hoard it in a vault. You've got to
taste it; you've got to use it. The more you use
the more you have...that's the miracle of it!

Kyle Samuel Crichton

The greatest thing is, at any moment,
to be willing to give up who we are
in order to become all that we can become.

Max De Pree

There is absolutely no pain in change or growth.
The pain is in the resistance
to the change or growth.

Bob Earll

May You Always Have...

*A*dventures to enrich your soul.
*B*lessings showered upon you.
*C*ourage to be yourself.
*D*reams that come true.
*E*nthusiasm to fuel your passions.
*F*amily, friends, and faith.
*G*reat things to look forward to.
*H*ealth to live long and prosper.
*I*magination to soar on wings.
*J*oy to color your thoughts.
*K*ind words to share.
*L*aughter to brighten your days.
*M*emories to keep you warm.

*N*ew horizons to explore.
*O*pportunities to grow.
*P*eace in your heart.
*Q*uestions to ponder.
*R*everence for life.
*S*trength to overcome adversity.
*T*ime to say "I love you."
*U*nderstanding to care.
*V*alues to guide you.
*W*ealth enough to share.
*X*uberance for your xistence.
*Y*outhfulness of spirit.
*Z*est to make a difference.

© *Meiji Stewart*

74

I am not afraid of storms, for I am learning
how to sail my ship. *Louisa May Alcott*

If it is to be, it is up to me.

E. Wilford Edmar

There's no feeling quite like the one you get when you get to the truth: You're the captain of the ship called you. You're setting the course, the speed, and you're out there on the bridge, steering.

Carl Frederick

Nothing adventured, nothing attained.

How wonderful it is that nobody need wait a single moment before starting to improve the world.

Anne Frank

Begin doing what you want to do now. We are not living in eternity. We have only this moment, sparkling like a star in our hand— and melting like a snowflake.

Marie Beynon Ray

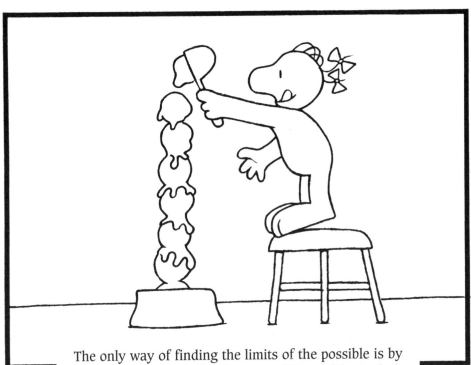

The only way of finding the limits of the possible is by going beyond them into the impossible. *Arthur C. Clarke*

First, when everybody tells you that you are being idealistic or impractical, consider the possibility that everybody could be wrong about what is right for you. Look inside yourself the way nobody else can. Will the pursuit of your dream hurt anybody? Do you stand at least a fair chance of success? If you fail, will you be seriously damaged or merely embarrassed? If you succeed, will it change your life for the better? When you can persuade yourself that your dream is worthwhile and achievable—then say thank you to the doubters and take the plunge....How much better to know that we have dared to live our dreams than to live our lives in a lethargy of regret.

Gilbert E. Kaplan

80

Dreams are the seedlings of reality. *James Allen*

Don't compromise yourself. You are all you've got.

Janis Joplin

If a man is called to be a street sweeper,
he should sweep streets as Michelangelo painted,
or Beethoven composed music, or Shakespeare wrote
poetry. He should sweep streets so well that
all the hosts of heaven and earth will pause to say,
here lived a great street sweeper
who did his job well.

Martin Luther King Jr.

This above all: to thine own self be true.... *William Shakespeare*

People must learn to gather adventures and experiences rather than things or possessions. Possessions will burden you, but adventures are memories which will enrich your soul and they will last forever.

Alfred A. Montapert

Don't smoke too much, drink too much, eat too much or work too much. We're all on the road to the grave—but there's no reason to be in the passing lane.

Robert Orben

Man who waits for roast duck to fly into mouth
must wait very, very long time. *Chinese Proverb*

It's so hard when I have to,
and so easy when I want to.

Sondra Anice Barnes

I have done my best and that is about all the
philosophy of living that one needs.

Lin Yutang

Where the soul is full of peace and joy,
outward surroundings and circumstances are
of comparatively little account.

Hannah Whitall Smith

The indispensable first step to getting the
things you want out of life is this:
decide what you want.

Ben Stein

Twenty years from now you will be more disappointed by the things that you didn't do than by the things you did. So throw off the bowlines. Sail away from the safe harbor. Catch the trade winds in your sail. Explore. Dream. Discover.

Mark Twain

Remember that you are unique. If that is not fulfilled,
then something wonderful has been lost. *Martha Graham*

If I have the belief that I can do it,
I shall surely acquire the capacity to
do it even if I may not have it at the beginning.

Mahatma Gandhi

You must understand the whole of life,
not just one little part of it. That is why
you must read, that is why you must look at
the skies, that is why you must sing and dance,
and write poems, and suffer, and understand,
for all that is life.

J. Krishnamurti

You know, of course, that it is never too late to begin. Why, Grandma Moses didn't start her painting career until she was seventy-six. *Carrie Bethard*

Cultivate your garden. Do not depend upon teachers to educate you...follow your own bent, pursue your curiosity bravely, express yourself, make your own harmony.

Will Durant

Pure and simple, any person who is enjoying life is a success.

William Feather

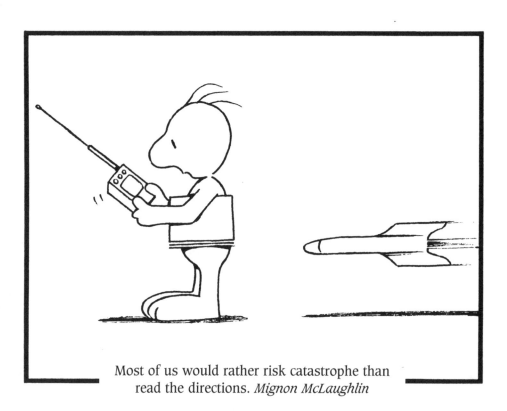

Most of us would rather risk catastrophe than
read the directions. *Mignon McLaughlin*

First I was dying to finish high school and start college. And then I was dying to finish college and start working. And then I was dying to marry and have children. And then I was dying for my children to grow old enough for school so I could return to work. And then I was dying to retire. And now I am dying...and suddenly I realize I forgot to live.

If one advances confidently in the direction of his dreams, and endeavors to live his life which he has imagined, he will meet success unexpected in common hours. *Henry David Thoreau*

People who make a living doing something
they don't enjoy wouldn't even be happy with a
one-day work week.

Duke Ellington

If you are afraid for your future,
you don't have a present.

James Petersen

One of these days is none of these days. *H. G. Bohn*

Just don't give up trying to do what you really want to do. Where there is love and inspiration, I don't think you can go wrong.

Ella Fitzgerald

Are you in earnest? Then seize this very minute. What you can do, or dream you can, begin it; Boldness has genius, power and magic in it; only engage and then the mind grows heated; Begin, and then the work will be completed.

Johann Wolfgang von Goethe

Most of the things worth doing in the world had been declared impossible before they were done. *Louis D. Brandeis*

What do you want to do?
What do you want to be?
What do you want to have?
Where do you want to go?
Who do you want to go with?
How the hell do you plan to get there?
Write it down. Go do it.
Enjoy it. Share it.
It doesn't get much simpler or better than that.

Lee Iacocca

No one should negotiate their dreams.
Dreams must be free to flee and fly high.
You should never agree to
surrender your aspirations.

Jesse Jackson

To change one's life: Start immediately.
Do it flamboyantly. No exceptions.

William James

Happiness Is...

*A*dventures in self-discovery.

*B*eing true to yourself.

*C*reating a life you love.

*D*isposition not circumstance.

*E*njoying what you have.

*F*inding balance.

*G*rowing friendships.

*H*elping others.

an *I*nside job, go within.

a *J*ourney of the heart.

*K*nowing when to let go.

*L*earning from your mistakes.

*M*aking the best of any situation.

*N*ot taking things personally.

*O*ptional, so is misery.

*P*rogress not perfection.

the *Q*uality of your thoughts.

*R*everence for body, mind, and spirit.

*S*pending time with loved ones.

*T*oday well lived.

*U*nderstanding how precious life is.

*V*aluing feelings and needs.

*W*hatever makes your heart sing.

*X*pressing your truth lovingly.

*Y*our choice, if not now, when?

*Z*zzzzzz's, a good night's sleep.

© *Meiji Stewart*

Happiness is a thing to be practiced, like the violin.
John Lubbock

The saddest words of tongue or pen are
these four words—it might have been.

Oliver Wendell Holmes

Let us endeavor to live that when we
come to die even the undertaker will be sorry.

Mark Twain

The only road to success is a road full of potholes and adversity, but through this adversity comes opportunity. *Jerry Colangelo*

This is the best day the world has ever seen.
Tomorrow will be better.

R. A. Campbell

The song I came to sing remains unsung.
I have spent my life stringing and
unstringing my instrument.

Rabindranath Tagore

If my doctor told me that I had only six minutes to live...I'd type a little faster. *Isaac Asimov*

I am an optimist. It does not seem
too much use being anything else.

Winston Churchill

We cannot tell what may happen to us
in the strange medley of life. But we can decide
what happens in us, how we take it, what we do
with it—and that is what really counts in the end.

Joseph Fort Newton

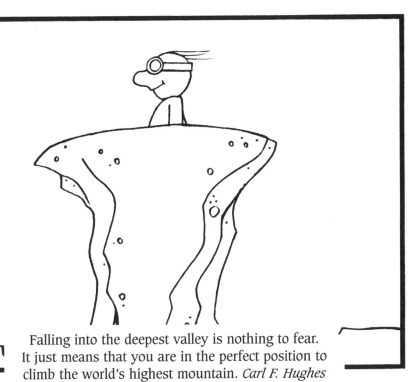

Falling into the deepest valley is nothing to fear.
It just means that you are in the perfect position to
climb the world's highest mountain. *Carl F. Hughes*

No age or time of life,
no position or circumstance,
has a monopoly on success.
Any age is the right age to start doing!

If you think you can, you can.
And if you think you can't, you're right.

Mary Kay Ash

The Wright brothers flew right through the smoke screen of impossibility. *Charles Kettering*

When one door closes another opens.
Expect that new door to reveal even greater
wonders and glories and surprises.
Feel yourself grow with every experience.
And look for the reason for it.

Eileen Caddy

The odds are with us if we keep on trying.

Keith De Green

If at first you don't succeed, try looking in the wastebasket for the instructions. *Ann Landers*

I would rather live in a world where my life is surrounded by mystery than live in a world so small that my mind could comprehend it.

Harry Emerson Fosdick

Why not? is a slogan for an interesting life.

Mason Cooley

Once you make a decision,
the universe conspires to make it happen.

Ralph Waldo Emerson

Our higher purpose is what we came here
on a soul level to do. We are born with specific
interests, talents, and abilities to fulfill that purpose.

Shakti Gawain

Keep a daily diary of your dreams,
goals and accomplishments. If your life is
worth living, it's worth recording.

Marilyn Grey

The good old days were never that good,
believe me. The good new days are today,
and better days are coming tomorrow.
Our greatest songs are still unsung.

Hubert H. Humphrey

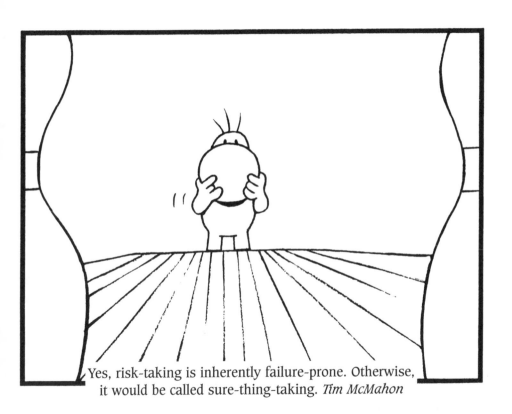

Yes, risk-taking is inherently failure-prone. Otherwise, it would be called sure-thing-taking. *Tim McMahon*

How we live, how we feel, what we think and what we become all depend on personal decisions. You are the master of your life. You can choose to celebrate life, live fully and live healthfully. Health is a choice! Happiness is a choice! Peace is a choice! And enthusiasm is the elixir that generates change, nourishes the body and feeds the soul.

Susan Smith Jones

The great composer does not set to work because he is
inspired, but becomes inspired because he is working.
Beethoven, Wagner, Bach, and Mozart settled down day after
day to the job in hand with as much regularity as an
accountant settles down each day to his figures. They didn't
waste time waiting for inspiration. *Ernest Newman*

It is good to have an end to journey towards;
but it is the journey that matters, in the end.

Ursula K. Le Guin

You can be anything you set out to be,
but first you must set out.

Margaret Mead

Discover day-to-day excitement. *Charles Baudelaire*

I've learned, the hard way, that some
poems don't rhyme, and some stories don't
have a clear beginning, middle, and end.
Life is about not knowing, having to change,
taking the moment and making the best of it,
without knowing what's going to happen next.
Delicious ambiguity.

Gilda Radner

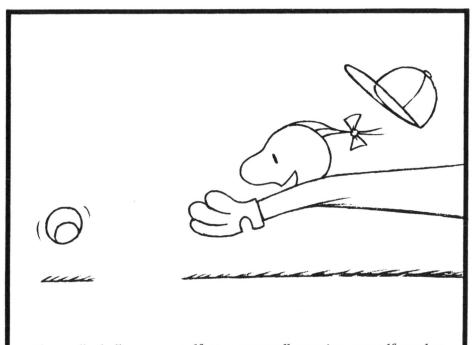

Above all, challenge yourself. You may well surprise yourself at what strengths you have, what you can accomplish. *Cecile M. Springer*

Honor your challenges, for those spaces that you label as dark are actually there to bring you more light.

Sanaya Roman

Only when we are no longer afraid do we begin to live.

Dorothy Thompson

The doors we open and close each day
decide the lives we live. *Flora Whittemore*

My favorite thing is to go where I've never been.

Diane Arbus

I am imagination.
I can see what the eyes cannot see.
I can hear what the ears cannot hear.
I can feel what the heart cannot feel.

Peter Nivio Zarlenga

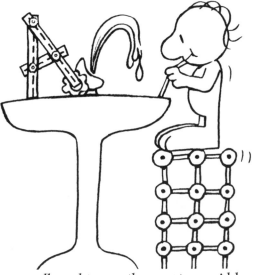

If children were allowed to run the country, we'd have soda flowing out of the drinking fountains, bridges built with Tinkertoys, Styrofoam airliners, and bad countries would have to play by themselves. *Walter Wandheim*

You can't help getting older,
but you don't have to get old.
New dreams, new works in progress—
that's the ticket for a long and happy ride.

George Burns

Why compare yourself with others?
No one in the entire world can do
a better job of being you than you.

Susan Carlson

Creativity is inventing, experimenting,
growing, taking risks, breaking rules,
making mistakes, and having fun.

Mary Lou Cook

How things look on the outside of us
depends on how things are on the inside of us.

Parks Cousins

Success Is...

Attitude, more than aptitude.

Being happy with who you are.

Cultivating, body, mind, and spirit.

Discovering that heaven is within.

Embracing the unknown with enthusiasm.

Facing fear, finding faith.

Giving, without remembering.

Here now, breathe into each moment.

Inside you, not in people, places, or things.

Journeying, from the head to the heart.

Knowing your beliefs create your experiences.

Letting go, and going with the flow.

Making time, for family, friends, and forgiveness.

Never ever giving up, on your hopes and dreams.

Opening your heart to magnificent possibilities.

Passion, playfulness, and peace of mind.

Quiet time, the key to inspired living.

Receiving, without forgetting.

Seeking answers, questioning beliefs.

Trusting, in the beauty of your feelings and needs.

Understanding, the best you can do is always enough.

a **V**erb, choreograph your dance with destiny.

Willingness, to learn from everything that happens.

Xpressing yourself, be the hero of your own story.

Yours to define, how do you want to be remembered?

Zestful living, loving, and laughing.

© *Meiji Stewart*

130

Success is never the result of spontaneous combustion.
You must set yourself on fire. *Arnold Glasgow*

There is a tremendous power in positive thinking.
When you expect the best, you literally create a
thought field that magnetizes that which
you desire. Like attracts like.

Douglas Bloch

Adventure is worthwhile in itself.

Amelia Earhart

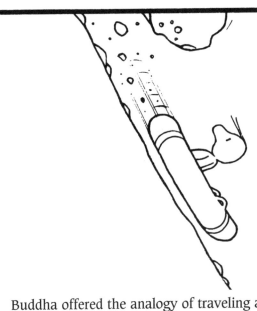

Buddha offered the analogy of traveling across a river on a raft. Once you get to the other side of the waterway, you must leave the raft on the river. It will do you no good to hang the raft on your back and carry it up the mountain. Leave it where you got it, and continue on your journey unimpeded.

Life does not accommodate you, it shatters you.
It is meant to and couldn't do it better.
Every seed destroys its container or else
there would be no growth, no fruition.

Florida Scott Maxwell

If I had my life to live over, I would start barefoot earlier in the spring and stay that way later in the fall. I would go to more dances. I would ride more merry-go-rounds. I would pick more daisies.

Nadine Stair

Joy is not in things; it is in us. *Richard Wagner*

The privilege of a lifetime is being who you are.

Joseph Campbell

To be nobody but yourself in a world which is doing
its best, day and night, to make you like everybody
else is to fight the hardest battle which any human
being can fight...but never stop fighting!

e. e. cummings

It is the simple things of life that make living worthwhile,
the sweet fundamental things such as love and duty, work
and rest, and living close to nature. *Laura Ingalls Wilder*

First say to yourself what you would be,
and then do what you have to do.

Epictetus

Don't part company with your ideals.
They are anchors in a storm.

Arnold Glasgow

138

Are you going places or just being taken? *H. F. Hendricks*

What you do is more important than
how much you make, and how you feel about it
is more important than what you do.

Jerry Gillies

What's important is
finding out what works for you.

Henry Moore

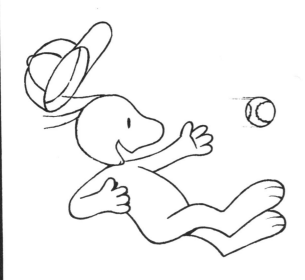

When we give it our all, we can live with ourselves—
regardless of the results. *William Wordsworth*

Here is the test
to find whether your mission on earth
is finished: If you're alive, it isn't.

Richard Bach

Believe nothing, no matter where you read it,
or who said it...unless it agrees with your own
reason and your own common sense.

Buddha

My dog and cat have taught me
a great lesson in life...shed a lot.

Susan Carlson

Who you are is a necessary step
to being who you will be.

Emmanuel

We will discover the nature of our particular genius when we stop trying to conform to our own or to other people's models, learn to be ourselves, and allow our natural channel to open.

Shakti Gawain

Life's most persistent and urgent question is: What are you doing for others?

Martin Luther King Jr.

You cannot prevent the birds of sorrow from flying over your head, but you can prevent them from building nests in your hair. *Chinese Proverb*

Dreams come a size too big so that
we can grow into them.

Josie Bisset

Hide not your talents, they for use were made.
What's a sundial in the shade?

Benjamin Franklin

We can't fly till we let go of the dirt.

It's not who we are that holds us back,
it's who we think we're not.

Michael Nolan

The greatest crime in the world is not developing
your potential. When you do what you do best,
you are helping not only yourself, but the world.

Roger Williams

We are given one life, we have one span to live it. We can wait for circumstances to make up our minds or we can decide to act, and in acting, live. *Omar Bradley*

You are never given a wish without also
being given the power to make it true.

Richard Bach

A tulip doesn't strive to impress anyone.
It doesn't struggle to be different than a rose.
It doesn't have to. It is different. And there's room
in the garden for every flower.

Marianne Williamson

Choose a job you love, and you will never
have to work a day in your life. *Confucius*

There are people who put their dreams in a little box and say, Yes, I've got dreams, of course, I've got dreams. Then they put the box away and bring it out once in a while to look in it, and yep, they're still there. These are great dreams, but they never even get out of the box. It takes an uncommon amount of guts to put your dreams on the line, to hold them up and say, How good or bad am I? That's where the courage comes in.

Erma Bombeck

My life is my message.

Mahatma Gandhi

Slow down and enjoy life.
It's not only the scenery you miss by going
too fast—you also miss the sense of
where you are going and why.

Eddie Cantor

For all that has been, Thanks.
For all that will be, Yes.

Dag Hammarskjöld

Go as far as you can see,
and when you get there you will see farther.

Orison Swett Marden

Take a chance! All life is a chance. The person who goes farthest is generally the one who is willing to do and dare. The "sure thing" boat never gets far from shore. *Dale Carnegie*

Little gift books, big messages

8313

6608

6456

6460

Little gift books, big messages

6458

6568

6569

6566

Little gift books, big messages

6457

6570

1737

1736

About the Author

Meiji Stewart has created other gift books, designs, and writings that may be of interest to you. Please visit www.puddledancer.com or call 1-877-EMPATHY (1-877-367-2849) for more information about any of the items listed below.

(1) **Hazelden/Keep Coming Back** - Over two hundred gift products, including greeting cards, wallet cards, bookmarks, magnets, bumper stickers, gift books, and more. (Free catalog available from Hazelden at 1-800-328-9000.)

(2) **ABC Writings** - Titles include *Children Are, Children Need, Creativity Is, Dare To, Fathers Are, Friends Are, Grandparents, Great Teachers, Happiness Is, I Am, Life Is, Loving Families, May You Always Have, Mothers Are, Recovery Is, Soulmates, Success Is,* and many more works in progress. Many of these ABC writings are available as posters (from Portal Publications) at your favorite poster and gift store, or directly from Hazelden on a variety of gift products.

(3) ***Nonviolent Communication: A Language of Compassion*** by Marshall Rosenberg (from PuddleDancer Press) - Jack Canfield (*Chicken Soup for the Soul* author) says, "I believe the principles and techniques in this book can literally change the world—but more importantly, they can change the quality of your life with your spouse, your children, your neighbors, your co-workers, and everyone else you interact with. I cannot recommend it highly enough." Available from Hazelden and your local and online bookstores. For more information about the Center for Nonviolent Communication call 1-800-255-7696 or visit www.cnvc.org

■ HAZELDEN®
Keep Coming Back™

Complimentary Catalog Available
Hazelden: P.O. Box 176, Center City, MN 55012-0176
1-800-328-9000   www.hazelden.org

**Hazelden/Keep Coming Back titles available from your
favorite bookstore:**

Relax, God Is in Charge	ISBN 1-56838-377-0
Keep Coming Back	ISBN 1-56838-378-9
Children Are Meant to Be Seen and Heard	ISBN 1-56838-379-7
Shoot for the Moon	ISBN 1-56838-380-0
When Life Gives You Lemons…	ISBN 1-56838-381-9
It's a Jungle Out There!	ISBN 1-56838-382-7
Parenting…Part Joy…Part Guerrilla Warfare	ISBN 1-56838-383-5
God Danced the Day You Were Born	ISBN 1-56838-384-3
Happiness Is an Inside Job	ISBN 1-56838-385-1
Anything Is Possible	ISBN 1-56838-386-X
Follow Your Dreams	ISBN 1-56838-514-5
Friends	ISBN 1-56838-515-3

Acknowledgments
Every effort has been made to find the copyright owner of the material used.
However, there are a few quotations that have been impossible to trace, and we
would be glad to hear from the copyright owners of these quotations so that
acknowledgment can be recognized in any future edition.